mazes & follies

Chris
Maybe some ideas
for your next
UK trip!
S & S x

mazes & follies

adrian fisher

Publication in this form copyright © Jarrold Publishing 2004
Text copyright © Adrian Fisher
The moral right of the author has been asserted
Series editor Jenni Davis
Designed by Mark Buckingham
Pictures researched by Jenni Davis

A CIP catalogue for this book is available from the British Library.

Published by:
Jarrold Publishing
Healey House, Dene Road, Andover, Hampshire, SP10 2AA
www.britguides.com

Set in Gill Sans Light
Printed in Singapore

ISBN 1-84165-142-7   1/04

Pitkin is an imprint of Jarrold Publishing, Norwich

contents

introduction   6

mazes   8

the spiritual quest   10

the grand design   18

amazingly good fun   30

follies   42

utter madness   44

the art of illusion   54

gracing the landscape   66

useful addresses   78

index   79

acknowledgements   80

introduction

The Temple of Ancient
Virtue at Stowe
Landscape Gardens,
Buckinghamshire.
The mizmaze (left)
on St Catherine's Hill,
Winchester, Hampshire.

Mazes and follies are two forms of landscape feature that have become quintessentially English. The country revels in the sheer diversity of her mazes, while many of her most notable follies – sometimes classically elegant, often completely bizarre – simply have no counterpart anywhere else in the world. Both are sophisticated acts of defiance against the remorseless forward march of the 'rational' world, which sometimes seems destined to sacrifice anything that might be perceived as beautiful in favour of what is merely functional.

How refreshing to find things that shake a fist at this inexorable pace of 'progress'! They inspire us to stand back and reflect that perhaps, with a timely review and change of direction, we could more richly fulfil our life's goals and ambitions.

mazes

A maze is deliberately designed to be the longest route from A to B. It is the antidote to the life's work of every road-traffic engineer, whose challenge is to get everyone from A to B as

quickly as possible. The engineer's vocation is destined to disappointment, since our society responds with mute persistence by spending exactly the same amount of time travelling each year, but simply covering greater distances. Why go anywhere at all? Why not take your friends and loved ones into a maze — and find yourself and each other!

The laurel maze at Glendurgan Garden, Cornwall, was planted in 1833.

mazes the spiritual quest

THE LABYRINTH, WITH ITS SINGLE PATH LEADING FROM THE ENTRANCE TO THE GOAL AT THE CENTRE, IS DEEPLY SYMBOLIC OF MAN'S SPIRITUAL QUEST, AND HAS BEEN ONE OF MANKIND'S MOST ENDURING IMAGES FOR NEARLY 4,000 YEARS.

The Alkborough Maze, Lincolnshire (right). The bronze labyrinth (above) is on the altarpiece at Watts Chapel, Compton, Surrey.

For most of this time, there was just one pattern, the seven-ring classical labyrinth. It was carved in rockfaces, laid out on rocky shorelines using water-rounded boulders to define the sides of the paths, and cut in grass to create distinctive turf labyrinths.

Mazes, which only stretch back in history about 400 years, are characterized by junctions and decision points. By contrast, although seemingly confusing, the labyrinth offers no puzzle challenge, but is nonetheless fascinating – it is an allegorical journey, a rite of passage. Labyrinths sometimes represent the forward thread of time and thus portray the path of life from birth to death; as spiritual journeys, they take the journey beyond death to salvation and eternal life. In later Christian times, the medieval Church gave the labyrinth names such as 'Chemin de Jerusalem', symbolizing a pilgrimage to the Holy City.

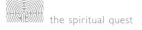

*The Hilton Turf Maze,
created in the mid
17th century.*

*The window maze in
Alkborough Church,
Lincolnshire (above).
The diagram (below)
shows the construction
of a classical labyrinth.*

The geometric form of construction of the classical labyrinth is simple and easily memorized, which greatly helped in its dissemination to all parts of the world over thousands of years. Start with a cross and four dots, and in turn connect each end of the cross to one of the dots; the resulting design has eight barriers, enclosing seven rings of paths.

Two of these classical labyrinths survive in England; one is in a private garden at Somerton, Oxfordshire, and the other – Britain's smallest turf maze – stands beside the road at Dalby, North Yorkshire. Later examples of turf labyrinths are based on a design introduced by the medieval Christian Church, and differ slightly from the classical labyrinth to distance them firmly from any lingering pagan associations.

The turf labyrinth on the village common of Hilton in Cambridgeshire has nine rings of paths instead of the conventional 11 rings of the medieval Christian pattern. This is possibly because when the labyrinth's creator, one William Sparrow, died in 1729 at the great age of 88, a central stone pillar set in a small grass circle was erected in his memory, and two rings of paths may have been lost in the process.

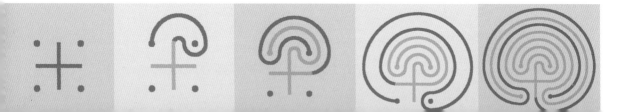

The Archbishop's Maze, Greys Court.

In his enthronement address on 25 March 1980 in Canterbury Cathedral, Archbishop Robert Runcie spoke of a maze: 'I had a dream of a maze. There were some people very close to the centre, but they could not find a way through. Just outside the maze others were standing. They were further away from the heart of the maze, but they would be there sooner than the party that fretted and fumed inside.'

This sermon inspired the creation of the Archbishop's Maze at Greys Court, Oxfordshire. The maze abounds in Christian symbolism: its cruciform shape, image of the Crown of Thorns, seven days of Creation, nine hours of Agony and twelve Apostles. At the centre, a simple Roman cross of Bath stone is laid within an elaborate Byzantine cross of blue Westmorland stone. These proclaim the reconciliation between East and West, Catholic and Protestant, Roman and Orthodox – a vital aspect of Robert Runcie's life's work. In one sense the maze is a puzzle, and there are various junctions with choices to be made. However, by crossing straight over each diamond-shaped thorn, one walks the entire length of the maze; this route represents the Christian path of life.

*The pavement maze
at Ely Cathedral.*

*The labyrinth roof boss
in St Mary Redcliffe
Church (above); the
Maze of the Mysteries
of the Gospel,
Wyck Rissington
Church (below).*

Although early labyrinths were very much a feature of the natural world, they eventually began to appear within sacred buildings as the symbolism was adopted by the Christian Church.

Ely Cathedral has a delightful pavement labyrinth, the only one of its kind in Britain, laid out by Sir George Gilbert Scott in 1870. The design is unusual, since it does not possess the internal rotational symmetry characteristic of medieval Christian labyrinths. The labyrinth, picked out in black and white stone, lies just inside the doors under the west tower and has a path length of 65.5m (215ft), precisely the height of the tower above it.

Not all labyrinths in churches can be walked, however. The 15th-century labyrinth in St Mary Redcliffe Church, Bristol, for example, takes the form of a beautifully gilded carved roof boss, only 20cm (8in) in diameter, set into the ceiling above the north aisle. Similarly, the stunning 19th-century labyrinths in the Watts Chapel in Compton, Surrey, are set into corbels and altar decorations, while on the north aisle wall of Wyck Rissington Church, Gloucestershire, is a wall mosaic replica of a hedge maze – the Maze of the Mysteries of the Gospel – that graced the rectory garden for 30 years.

mazes # the grand design

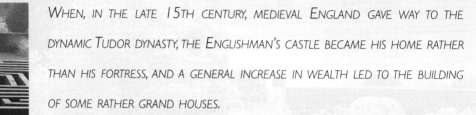

The formal maze at Hatfield House in Hertfordshire (above and right).

WHEN, IN THE LATE 15TH CENTURY, MEDIEVAL ENGLAND GAVE WAY TO THE DYNAMIC TUDOR DYNASTY, THE ENGLISHMAN'S CASTLE BECAME HIS HOME RATHER THAN HIS FORTRESS, AND A GENERAL INCREASE IN WEALTH LED TO THE BUILDING OF SOME RATHER GRAND HOUSES.

At this point also, the thoughts of their owners turned to planting gardens as an attractive setting for their desirable new residences. Knot gardens were popular with the Tudors, and retained an element of the functional medieval garden, as evergreen herbs were used to create the shape; and in time a variation appeared – the maze. Both were designed to be viewed from the upper windows of the house, and were wonderful to walk in, as brushing through the herbs released their scent. However, herbs needed a lot of attention, and eventually dwarf box – slow-growing but obligingly bushy and long-lived – was used instead.

Mazes were originally designed not to confuse, but merely as a means of taking a long walk in a small space. The concept of the puzzle maze, with its high hedges and challenging dead ends, arrived in England with King William of Orange, and – along with other types of maze – has become part of the grand garden design.

The hedge maze
at Longleat House;
(left) the maze at
Hampton Court Palace.

Hampton Court Palace in Surrey has the oldest surviving hedge maze, planted when the gardens were laid out for King William of Orange in the late 17th century. Its odd trapezoid shape was dictated by paths running across the adjoining 'Wilderness'. The maze later escaped the hand of 'Capability' Brown, the Royal Gardener with a penchant for making somewhat sweeping changes, on the express orders of King George III.

Hampton Court set the scene for hedge mazes as an element of garden design – even if it took a while for others to catch up. The hedge maze at Longleat House in Wiltshire was designed in 1978 and is one of the largest in the world. This maze is seriously sophisticated – six bridges create a three-dimensional puzzle, spiral junctions add confusion by repetition, and although elongated fork junctions help visitors to 'conserve their momentum', the whirling lines and lack of any rectangular grid add further disorientation.

'They all got crazy at last, and sang out for the keeper, and the man came and climbed up the ladder outside, and shouted out directions to them. But all their heads were, by this time, in such a confused whirl that they were incapable of grasping anything …'

Jerome K. Jerome, on the visit to Hampton Court Maze in *Three Men in a Boat*

*The maze in the Tudor
Garden at Hever Castle;
the Tudor Rose maze
(right) at Kentwell Hall.*

Mazes are a fun way of keeping history alive, and two very different mazes ensure that the flamboyant Tudors continue to make their mark, 400 years after the line died out.

Filling the main courtyard of Kentwell Hall in Long Melford, Suffolk, the highly entertaining Tudor Rose maze was built with 27,000 red and white paving bricks. Fifteen diamonds of etched brick, decorated with symbols representing the Tudor dynasty, are set into the design. The five separate progressions through the maze, from the five outer thorns to the centre, echo the internal rotational symmetry hidden within classical and medieval Christian labyrinths. Alternatively, the rose becomes a three-dimensional puzzle maze, by observing junctions and flyovers indicated by the brick paths, and at the centre is a giant chessboard.

A Tudor atmosphere also prevails at Hever Castle, Kent, where Henry VIII, becoming anxious to sire that elusive son and heir, came to court his second wife, the ill-fated Anne Boleyn. An American millionaire, William Waldorf Astor, bought the 13th-century castle in 1903, and had the square hedge maze installed – along with a set of topiary chessmen – in the Tudor garden.

The celebratory Marlborough Maze, Blenheim Palace (left and right).

Blenheim Palace at Woodstock, Oxfordshire, was given to John Churchill, First Duke of Marlborough, by Queen Anne in recognition of his military success against the French at Blenheim in 1704, the first of four great victories in the War of the Spanish Succession. It was certainly quite a reward, somewhat negated by the fact that Marlborough fell out of favour with the queen, the funds that were promised failed to arrive and the Duke was left in a state of financial embarrassment.

Nonetheless, the house, built by Sir John Vanbrugh, was decorated by the leading craftsmen of the day. It was one of these, the fabulously talented carver Grinling Gibbons, who inspired the design of the Marlborough Maze, created to celebrate the battle at Blenheim, a great highlight in English history. Seen from above, the lines of the yew hedges portray pyramids of cannon balls, a cannon firing, and the air filled with banners, flags and the sound of trumpets, a reflection of Gibbons' stone sculpture on the palace roof depicting the Panoply of Victory. Two wooden bridges create a three-dimensional puzzle, and give tantalizing views over the world's largest symbolic hedge maze.

Mazes are often created in the midst of the most glorious surroundings, reflecting the beauty and grandeur of the castles and houses themselves.

The maze at Chatsworth House in Derbyshire has one of the most magnificent settings of any hedge maze in the world, surrounded by mature Wellingtonias, raised grass banks and paths on all sides, and stone bridges at each end. The maze, which was planted in 1962 but echoes an earlier design, acts like a magnet in the landscape, drawing visitors irresistibly through various parts of the garden.

Leeds Castle, arguably 'the loveliest castle in the world', is

Chatsworth House maze (right); Leeds Castle maze (above) and the route to its goal (below), an underground grotto at the centre.

set on two Kentish lake islands and has been inhabited by several queens of England, the first of which was Queen Eleanor, wife of Edward I. The maze is itself a topiary castle with castellated yew hedges, an entrance bridge and a central tower. Once this goal is reached, a queen's crown and a chalice, laid out in the hedges, are visible from the stone parapet; looking down, visitors see splashing water and light below, and descend to discover an underground grotto decorated

with seashells and statues. An underground passage leads to a flooded cave, the seat of the nymph of the grotto, and back to the outside world.

The turf maze at Chenies Manor House; the maze in the Tudor garden at Hatfield House (above).

Many of the modern mazes found in the grounds of old country houses are recycled versions of much older designs, lovingly recreated to be enjoyed all over again.

The recreated Tudor garden in front of the Old Palace at Hatfield House in Hertfordshire has a square hedge maze only a few inches high, in the parterre style. Planted in dwarf box (*Buxus sempervirens*), the design is based on engravings from the 16th century.

The wonderful atmosphere, evocative of an age when there was time to spare for quiet contemplation, would no doubt overcome any urge to hop over the hedges instead of following the paths they form, but in fact this maze was created to be observed only, not walked in.

The turf maze at Chenies Manor House, Buckinghamshire, was created in 1983, but the elegantly spiralling design is based on the depiction of an ornamental maze in the background of a painting dated 1573 of Edward, Lord Russell, the grandson of the first Earl of Bedford, who owned Chenies in the mid 16th century.

mazes amazingly good fun

*The Sun and Moon
Mazes at Longleat
House, Wiltshire.*

THE 19TH AND 20TH CENTURIES SAW MANY CHANGES — MORE WAYS OF GETTING

ABOUT, MORE LEISURE TIME, MORE MONEY AVAILABLE FOR HAVING FUN —

and these inspired the creation of ever more sophisticated forms of family entertainment. Zoos, wildlife parks, aquariums, hands-on science centres, children's museums, theme parks – you name it, they're out there. Mazes lend themselves to layer upon layer of pure, unadulterated enjoyment. Getting through a maze is fun in itself; getting through a maze that involves water, mirrors, a giant locomotive or a much-loved children's story is amazingly good fun. This is where reality is left far, far behind and one enters the glorious realm of fantasy. What better way to spend an hour or two than dodging between high hedges, wooden fences, wattle panels, a field of waving corn, a forest reflected in mirror after mirror, and know that one is part of a magical tale with an enticing goal to reach – the heart of the maze. Or to follow the endlessly flowing lines of a brick-path maze, or to stand before a mesmerizing waterfall and wonder how you will ever reach the maze beyond …

There is something irresistible about water, and entering a maze through a waterfall that magically parts as you enter adds an extra element of excitement to an already thrilling adventure. Add to that the romance and mystery of themes such as the ancient Celts and a bearded magician named Merlin, and fantasy is there at your fingertips.

A fantasy in itself, Legoland – near Windsor in Berkshire – has three mazes, the Celtic Maze, the Tudor Maze and the Nautical Maze. The only way into the Tudor Maze is through a waterfall, which cascades over a turreted paparet into a moat. To cross this moat, a bridge has been provided – but at the far end of the bridge, the waterfall blocks your way. This contrived paradox has an equally bizarre solution, since if you walk steadily towards the waterfall, it anticipates your arrival and lets you pass without getting wet. A similar paradox, leading into a mirrored grotto, lies in wait at Merlin's Magical Maze near Newquay in Cornwall.

The Celtic Maze at Legoland (above); the watery entrance to Legoland's Tudor Maze (right); Merlin's Magical Maze (far right) at Holywell Bay Fun Park near Newquay.

The Lappa Maze at the
Lappa Valley Railway.

A very unusual way to encourage small boys to live out their dream of being a train-driver is to let them loose in the Lappa Maze at the Lappa Valley Railway in St Newlyn, Cornwall. This brick-path representation of the world's first locomotive, which was built in 1804 by the Cornish inventor Richard Trevithick, is on a scale of eight times the size of the original engine. Trevithick's Tramroad Locomotive predated the more famous engines built by the Stephensons, such as *Locomotion* and *Rocket*.

The paths portray the vast flywheel and interacting pattern of cogs. On the driving wheels, children turn tightly to and fro between the meshing cogs until they get to the flywheel, where they can fling wide their arms and run in imitation of the whirling speed of its circumference. The goal is the centre of the small driving cog, reached by following the huge connecting rod from the pistons.

Hidden within the design are the giant letters 'T' for Trevithick and 'L' for Lappa, as well as the date 1804 in Roman figures – MDCCCIIII – and 'E.W.R.' for the East Wheal Rose Mine, beside which the maze is sited.

The Pirate Galleon
Maze at Tulleys Farm;
an artwork of the Saxon
Maze, Sonning Common
Herb Farm (left).

Most hedge mazes are planted with evergreens; they take a while to establish but, once established, they are there, exactly the same, summer and winter. Just occasionally, however, a maze is created from something completely different, something that dies off in the winter and leaps back to life in the spring – or even something that is planted in the spring, grows rapidly during the summer, and is harvested in the autumn, leaving just a memory once winter comes.

Maize mazes are amazing because a new design can be created every year by cutting pathways into a huge cornfield. At Tulleys Farm in West Sussex, there has been a Dragon Maze and a Pirate Galleon Maze, a Castle Maze and a Wild West Maze, a Jungle Maze and a Sea Monster Maze, each perfect in every detail – from a skull and crossbones on a straining sail, to the turreted towers of a fantasy fortress flying on a cumulus cloud.

At Sonning Common Herb Farm in Oxfordshire is a Saxon Maze planted in deciduous beech. Four mythical sea creatures, which were inspired by a depiction in an illuminated manuscript dating from the 8th century, make up the wonderful curving lines of this intriguing maze. In the eye of each creature is one of the herbs that were sacred to the Saxons.

The Magical Mirror Maze at Wookey Hole Caves; King Arthur's Mirror Maze, Longleat House (above).

A fascinating variation on the maze theme is one where 'they do it with mirrors'. Unlike a hedge or brick-path maze, where the challenge lies in the twists and turns and dead ends, a mirror maze is all illusion and deception. The eye is tricked and the brain deceived – nothing is what it seems! Throw in a little fantasy, and fun is bound to follow.

Enter King Arthur's Mirror Maze, at Longleat House in Wiltshire, in the guise of a knight on a quest and journey through an enchanted forest. Excalibur, the legendary sword in the stone, tantalizingly appears, rises and disappears again. Find yourself jumping in alarm at wild sounds, a tolling bell, swirling fog, flashes of lightning and crashing thunder, the occasional glimpse of a Green Man, half-hidden in the branch of a tree … Eventually you reach the ruined chapel, where – if you are pure in heart (or simply rather clever) – you may discover the Holy Grail.

At Wookey Hole Caves in Somerset, the Magical Mirror Maze was inspired by portable mirror mazes found in travelling fairgrounds a hundred years ago, but on a much grander scale. There appears to be an almost infinite number of choices to be made, but in reality there is only one path …

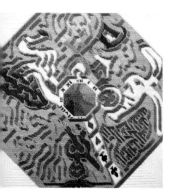

Veronica's Maze at Parham Park; an embroidery of the Alice in Wonderland Maze at Hurn (above).

Veronica's Maze at Parham Park, West Sussex, and the Alice in Wonderland Maze at Hurn, Dorset, demonstrate that embroidery can inspire a maze and a maze can inspire embroidery!

The maze of brick paths set into the lawn at Parham is based on the design of an ancient embroidery that hangs over the Great Bed in the principal bedroom in the house. Nowhere in this restful, flowing design is there a staight line, and the maze is one-way – once you've started walking, you must keep going forward, taking only gentle forks and making no sharp turns.

The embroidery illustrated to the left, from Lewis Carroll's children's fantasy *Alice's Adventures in Wonderland*, really does exist as a hedge maze. Follow the paths and come across the book's characters in their topsy-turvy dream world – Alice, the Mad Hatter, the White Rabbit, the Gryphon, the Queen of Hearts, the Cheshire Cat, the Mock Turtle and the Dodo. At the centre of the maze the White Rabbit's pocket watch indicates four o'clock, perpetual teatime; and of course there's the giant teapot, with its sleeping Dormouse. Like the end of Alice's dream, visitors leave in a flurry of playing cards …

follies

A folly is a structure whose kudos increases the more seemingly useless it can be shown to be. An arch that leads nowhere, a triangular tower, a classical temple sitting incongruously

Ralph Allen's Sham Castle, Bath, Somerset.

in the English countryside … 'What misguided human effort,' we cry – and yet, what fun! So let us have inspiring monuments that capture the mood of a people, a nation, or mankind. Let us celebrate our vibrant lives through our inherent talents of wit, vitality, surprise and humour. Let us continue to use follies to play these joyful and monstrous jokes on the landscape!

utter madness

THERE ARE TYPICALLY THREE PLAYERS IN ANY ARTISTIC CREATION — THE OWNER, THE DESIGNER AND THE INTENDED VISITOR.

It is the owner who is central to this drama. The designer bends to the owner's will. Then, dear visitor, it's over to you.

It was owners unconstrained by mere practical details, whose flights of fancy collided with the financial means to realize their dreams, who truly set the mischievous Folly Demon loose on the landscape. Indeed, had they the faintest grasp of the financial and technical consequences of their architectural ambitions, even these eccentric personalities might have shied away from a course of action that sometimes brought destitution, despair and utter ruin upon themselves and those most dear to them.

What drives someone to pursue such a bizarre aspiration? Actually, no more than a whisker aside from the buccaneering playfulness of the true business entrepreneur, whether or not bearded and knighted as in our contemporary generation, who risks even his own life in such things as extreme hot-air balloon challenges. Considered this way, it is not so surprising that these rare rogue spirits so very often succeeded triumphantly in creating their improbable structures.

The skill is in knowing when to stop. And many of them never did!

In the days before one neighbour could impress another by driving a fast, expensive car, people were rather more inventive with their methods of getting noticed. They could, for example, erect a very tall Gothic clock tower within unmissable sight and sound of those frustrating individuals who had managed – somehow – to climb that little bit further up the ladder of social and financial success ...

The Abberley Clock Tower, Stourport-on-Severn; the interior (left) is as elegant as the exterior.

John Jones, who owned Abberley Hall, declared that he built the Abberley Clock Tower, perched prominently on top of Merritt's Hill near Stourport-on-Severn in Worcestershire, in memory of his father. However, it is common knowledge that this was just a ruse, and that his real motive was to impress the residents of nearby Witley Court, which was built by the first Lord Foley in the 18th century and had been home to such conspicuous aristrocrats as the Earl of Dudley and Queen Adelaide.

The elegant structure dates from 1883–4, when the great Victorian Gothic Revival was beginning to draw to a close. With its 20 bells, which can play more than 40 different tunes, the tower would certainly have made its presence felt …

*The House in the
Clouds, Thorpeness,
Suffolk; (left) the homely
sewage maceration
station at Hengistbury
Head (below).*

The House in the Clouds at Thorpeness in Suffolk carries off to perfection a splendid deception. It consists of a weatherboarded 1920s house, traditional in almost every detail including tall chimneys, steep roofs and distinctive windows. Its only unusual characteristic is that it is supported 12m (40ft) above the ground by a tall tower. From a distance, this gives the disconcerting impression of a very solid house floating weightlessly through the sky like a novelty hot-air balloon. In fact, it is a functional water tower with the tank camouflaged by this distinctive villa.

There are several other examples of camouflaged buildings in England, each installed by utility companies. At Hengistbury Head near Bournemouth, Dorset, a sewage maceration station is disguised as a bungalow, its garden apparently tended enthusiastically by its fictitious occupiers – the purpose is to preserve the idyllic character of the neighbourhood. Still in Dorset, at Poundbury near Dorchester, a classical pavilion offers a place to sit and admire the view towards Maiden Castle; the pavilion itself contains and conceals an electricity substation. In Green Lanes, North London, a joyfully extravagant mock castle, with a series of irregular towers of varying heights and styles, hides its true function as the Stoke Newington Pumping Station.

*The Triangular Lodge
at Rushton; King Alfred's
Tower, Stourhead (left).*

Part of the fun of follies is their sheer impracticality. A square structure has 130 per cent more floorspace than a triangular one, for want of adding 25 per cent to the number of walls.

Yet the moment we approach and examine the Triangular Lodge at Rushton, Northamptonshire, we encounter intense and earnest Christian symbolism, expressed with a remorseless and urgent determination. In this extraordinary representation of the Holy Trinity, 'three' is everywhere – for example, the three walls are each topped with three triangular gables, and its three floors are linked by a 33-step spiral staircase. Suddenly, out leaps the contemporary world of its creator, Sir Thomas Tresham, a Catholic landowner persecuted and imprisoned for holding firm to his beliefs in the reign of the staunchly Protestant Queen Elizabeth I – a world in which literal life-and-death outcomes were tearing apart the fabric of English society as the new faith struggled to suppress the old.

By comparison, the triangular King Alfred's Tower, part of Stourhead Gardens in Wiltshire, has no meaningful symbolism attached and is simply a folly, built for the stunning views from the top. Designed by Henry Flitcroft, it was completed in 1772 and stands on the spot where its namesake, King Alfred – 'the Great' in name and deed – raised his standard against the invading Danes in 870.

Haldon Belvedere; the surprises to be found within include a ballroom (below) and a spiral staircase (right).

Most follies are built with admiration in mind — either the folly itself is admired, or one climbs the folly to admire the view. Sometimes one can sit in them. Very rarely can one actually live in them.

A charming exception to this is Haldon Belvedere near Doddiscombsleigh in Devon, also known as Lawrence Castle. This Gothic extravaganza was built in 1788 by Sir Robert Palk — who had made his fortune through the East India Company and was reputedly one of the richest men of his day — as a memorial to his friend, Major-General Stringer Lawrence. Haldon's triangular plan, with its sturdy turrets at each corner and some rather grand first-floor Gothic Venetian windows, marks it out as a folly; yet it was designed to use as a home, or at least as unique guest accommodation — the Palk family used it to entertain their special guests, such as the king.

The interior of the folly is as decorative as the exterior, with ornate plasterwork, real marble and mahogany flooring. There is even a ballroom, should the urge overcome you to take a turn around the floor, and a spiral staircase leads to a roof terrace where — in classic tower-folly style — there are marvellous views to be admired …

the art of illusion

The Turkish Tent at Painshill Park, Surrey; this folly, originally dating from 1760, has been recreated with drapes made of fibreglass – the ultimate illusion.

SOME OF THE FINEST FOLLIES EMPLOY TRICKS AND ILLUSIONS THAT MATCH ANYTHING

ON THE THEATRICAL STAGE OR SILVER SCREEN.

Perhaps the folly is intended to give the impression of a large and substantial building, when in fact it is just a façade or a 'sham', or perhaps a building just one room deep, though wide and tall. It might be a castle that – unlike real castles, which were built for distinct military purposes and only fell into ruin when advanced technology rendered them obsolete – never had any military objective. This is what qualifies it as a folly.

In breathtakingly beautiful landscapes, a well-positioned sample of distinctive architecture can be used to convey a complete idea, such as a vision of Arcadia, or a glimpse of heavenly perfection on earth.

Illusions sometimes work not only at a distance, but also close up. When one can walk right up to the folly and climb up inside it, the excitement can still be powerful even if one knows all along that it was built as a folly.

The sham castle at Wimpole Hall; the Ruined Tower in Mount Edgcumbe Park (left).

There is something infinitely evocative about ruins ... a pathos, a drama, a sense of romance. But in order to become a romantic ruin, something has to be built, destroyed, gradually decayed over centuries – unless, of course, you skip a few hundred years and create a ready-made ruin. There are some wonderful examples of these to be found.

Stand in the window of the Saloon at Wimpole Hall in Cambridgeshire and your gaze is drawn inexorably through a frame of trees to a delectable sham castle. This Gothic tower, flanked by artistically 'crumbling' walls, was designed by Sanderson Miller and built by 'Capability' Brown in the second half of the 18th century.

The Ruined Tower in Mount Edgcumbe Park in Cornwall was created as a folly when it lay within the estate of the Edgcumbe family of Cotehele. Today, the estate has become a magnificent country park, with fine views across Plymouth Sound. The folly itself stirs up the imagination, as one ascends from one style of steps to another, through false 'ruined' walls and arches to its highest vantage point, which takes advantage of the steeply falling slope to maximum dramatic effect.

*Middleton Arch, on the
border between Essex
and Suffolk; Rousham
Folly, Steeple Aston,
Oxfordshire (right);
Creech Grange Arch,
Purbeck, Dorset (below).*

One thinks of an arch as being grand, triumphal, a glorious entrance. Or as being practical, strong, the most efficient structural device to support aqueducts and viaducts.

However, sometimes an arch is quite simply – a folly. Sitting in the middle of nowhere, for no apparent reason. You walk through it, and nothing has changed – there is no fanfare of trumpets, no feeling of awe that such delicate-looking arches can support a bridge to carry you safely over a deep ravine.

But, in fact, that arch has served another purpose – it's drawn your attention. Who could spot the delicately beautiful Middleton Arch, on the Essex-Suffolk border, and not stop to wonder exactly what it is doing there? Why is there a sturdy but austere structure of three completely pointless arches, sitting in splendid isolation on the Purbeck Hills above the Dorset coast? Why, near Steeple Aston in Oxfordshire, is there another flat structure with three arches, so substantial that it

needs hearty buttresses to support it, just planted in the middle of a field?

The answer is that all three are superb examples of what, in folly language, are described – succinctly but so perfectly – as 'eyecatchers'. The viewpoint often turns out to be an historic house, situated a mile or more away.

*Clavel's Folly, or
Kimmeridge Tower;
the Temple of Concord,
Audley End (left).*

The classical style of architecture lends itself beautifully to follies – authoritative, timeless, sometimes disintegrating a little …

Clavel's Folly at Kimmeridge on the Dorset coast is one of several follies built on dramatic coastlines. This one, more commonly known as 'Kimmeridge Tower', was designed in the 1820s as a summerhouse for the Reverend John Richards, who had inherited the Smedmore estate, on which the tower stands, in 1817. With its covered colonnade surrounding the circular tower, the folly certainly has the air of a remnant from an ancient civilization, but regrettably it was not designed this way – it is, in fact, in a very poor state of repair and alarmingly close to the rapidly crumbling cliff-edge.

The magnificent Temple of Concord at Audley End in Essex was designed by Robert William Brettingham in 1790 to celebrate the recovery of King George III from his first bout of apparent 'madness'. The original Temple of Concord, in Rome, was built to celebrate the concept of concord, or harmony, particularly between patricians and plebeians, so this was an interesting choice of symbolism. Was it a belated gesture on behalf of James I's Lord Treasurer, who built the palatial Audley End and was subsequently charged with embezzlement and disgraced?

The 'ruined' abbey at Painshill Park. A vineyard growing alongside adds to the impression that this was a working medieval abbey.

Some of the nation's most beautiful ruins are those of the abbeys that fell into disrepair after Henry VIII's ruthless dissolution in the mid 16th century. Fountains Abbey, Rievaulx Abbey, Hailes Abbey and so forth have inspired artists and poets alike – J.M.W. Turner's mellow, ivy-clad, sunlit ruins of Tintern Abbey, for example, have an almost ethereal quality.

Seemingly standing tall alongside these treasures of a gone but not forgotten age is the ruined abbey within Painshill Park, a glorious landscape garden in Surrey laid out between 1738 and 1773 by Charles Hamilton. The one awkward deficiency to prick this particular bubble is the fact that there was never an abbey here – these ruins, just one of several follies at Painshill, are a total sham. Seen from across a lake at twilight, one's mind's eye strains to detect monks gliding silently around their eternal domain. But no, it was just a trick of the light.

Today the park has been gloriously restored. According to the Alice-in-Wonderland system of values that we are applying to follies, this might seem to be a case of snatching defeat from the jaws of victory. Fortunately not. At Painshill, each vibrant and splendid folly still conveys its vigorous irreverence.

Leith Hill Tower;
Broadway Tower (above).

The principal purpose of a tower is to look out from it. Church towers and spires combine a vertical symbol of faith with a practical high point in which to hang bells, so that the sound can carry far and wide, summoning people to worship. In castles, towers are used primarily as defensive structures, but are also useful for spotting the approach of an enemy.

However, as follies, towers take on two new and enchanting roles – as viewpoints to be seen from, and as contrived landscape features to be looked at for pleasure. The more these pleasures are their only functions, the more joyful they are as follies.

Such a tower sits on top of Leith Hill in Surrey, the highest point in south-east England. This 'prospect tower' was built in 1765 in Gothic style by one Richard Hull, who thoughtfully provided small telescopes, 'not only for his own enjoyment, but for anyone else who wished to savour the fine views it has to offer'.

Another is Broadway Tower in Gloucestershire, built in 1797 by the Sixth Earl of Coventry for his wife, who apparently wanted to be able to see the tower – topped by a beacon – from her house in Worcester.

follies gracing the landscape

The classical landscape at Stourhead in Wiltshire contains a remarkable variety of follies; here, the Grass Bridge is seen in the foreground, while across the lake is the Pantheon.

THE ENGLISH CHARACTER AND TEMPERAMENT LENDS ITSELF TO FOLLIES AND GARDEN SURPRISES, JUST AS THE FERTILE CLIMATE PROVIDES THE GREATEST ENCOURAGEMENT TO ENGLISH GARDENERS, WHATEVER THEIR TALENT OR OTHERWISE.

One of the main influences for the creation of follies in England would have been the experience of travelling around Renaissance Europe, especially Italy, and seeing the opulence and imagination of the gardens and contrived landscapes. The wit of walking behind a semi-circular waterfall, as in the Tivoli Gardens near Rome, or seeing a complete house built on a distinct tilt, as in the Bomarzo Gardens near Viterbo, would have whipped up the desire to create further follies upon returning home.

Some of the greatest names in the history of English architecture, more usually associated with buildings such as churches and country estates, were responsible for designing these follies, including James Wyatt, Henry Flitcroft, Sir John Vanbrugh, James Gibbs and William Kent.

The Temple of Worthies, a display of pride in Britain at Stowe Landscape Gardens; Alexander Pope (left) is one of the 'worthies'.

To the north of Buckingham is Stowe, the quintessential landscape garden. The gardens were first laid out in the late 17th century, and during the 18th century were enlarged and remodelled, losing their air of formality in favour of a more naturalistic, yet still almost theatrical, feel. This landscape of grassy vistas, calm waters and woodland is graced with classical temples and pavilions, monuments and bridges.

Among these, the semi-circular Temple of British Worthies makes quite a statement. A central bust of Mercury – who conducted the souls of the blessed across the Styx to the Elysian Fields – is flanked by busts of 'members of the British nation thought worthy of being set in such exalted company'. To the left are men of contemplation – Inigo Jones, William Shakespeare, Francis Bacon, John Milton, John Locke, Isaac Newton and Sir Thomas Gresham, while to the right are men (and one woman) of action – King Alfred, the Black Prince, Elizabeth I, Walter Raleigh, Francis Drake, John Hampden and William III. At either end is a bust of a living hero of the time – the poet Alexander Pope and a Member of Parliament, Sir John Barnard, who shared the political views of Lord Cobham, Stowe's owner.

The landscape gardens at Stourhead in Wiltshire, laid out in the 18th century, establish their world-class reputation with a good deal of panache. Classical temples are dotted around the lake to entice at every twist and turn – the Pantheon, the Temple of Apollo, the Temple of Flora, the Temple of the Sun – reflecting the main house built in early Palladian style.

It is somewhat confusing, then, in the middle of all this grace and splendour (and having recently emerged, blinking a little, from a long tunnel grotto with a reclining nymph at its centre), to suddenly stumble upon a little rustic cottage, the sort you find in fairy tales. No Doric porticos or Corinthian capitals here – just an open-sided porch, a little chimney, and a row of Gothic windows with a little stone seat below, the better to admire the view.

'Mix a little foolishness with

your prudence: it's good to be

silly at the right moment.'

Horace, 65–88 BC

The Grass Bridge at Stourhead (far right) and the Palladian Bridge at Stowe cunningly disguise the dams beneath them.

Bridges are meant to be useful, providing a route across a river, a road, a railway ... but the grass covering the stone bridge at Stourhead turns this functional structure into something quite useless, since the grass is an impractical surface. The bridge qualifies in further ways as being useless since it goes nowhere, and the public are never allowed to cross it. Its only weakness in its claim to be a folly is that its arches conceal a dam, which enables water upstream to form a larger lake than would otherwise be created; however, this widely used device also helps this bridge qualify as a deception in the landscape.

There are bridges covering dams at numerous other places including Castle Howard, Longleat, Stowe and Wilton House – the latter two have outrageously grand Palladian bridges. The ceiling of the covered bridge at Stowe was inspired by a classical model at Palmyra and there are carved masks adorning the keystones. Ramps up to the bridge enabled carriages to be driven through the colonnade so that guests could enjoy the glorious – and thoughtfully contrived – views across to the Octagon Lake and the Elysian Fields.

*The Menagerie, named
after the zoo that was
once at Horton House,
Northamptonshire; today,
the only wild animals are
in the grotto (left).*

There are probably many people who are tempted to call their house 'The Menagerie' – pet dogs, cats, hamsters and rabbits can certainly give the impression that animals have taken over the family home.

Near Horton in Northamptonshire, the Second Earl of Halifax did just that, in the mid 18th century – or, at least, he built a folly, with a zoo attached that gave it its name, in the grounds of his mansion, Horton House. It was designed by Thomas Wright of Durham in the style of a Palladian palace, with a pavilion at either end, to be viewed from the main house across the valley.

The zoo has long gone, and although the folly's entrance is solemnly guarded by a statue of a handsome lion, it is in the shell-lined grotto beneath, added in the late 20th century, that the real menagerie is now to be found. Here, at the centre, we find Orpheus, who in Greek legend played his lyre so enchantingly that wild beasts were spellbound by his music – Cerberus the two-headed dog is certainly quite motionless, as are the lion, the panther, the monkey, the deer and the fabulous sea-monster, a figment of the designer's imagination.

Although the 18th-century 'Gothick' revival was rather frowned upon for being more to do with visual effect than with architectural accuracy, it was nonetheless perfect for folly design. Nowhere is this more apparent than at Painshill Park – here, an absolutely delightful Gothic temple sits on the crest of a steep grassy slope, where one stands on the brink of an abyss like an Olympic skier ready to cast forth down the Giant Jump. There is a decorative paved floor, and no doors or windows – just a series of slender pillars supporting elegant arches.

The ten-sided Gothic Folly at Painshill Park; the interior of 'The Castle' at Saltram (above).

'The Castle' at Saltram, Devon, was built in 1772 and has an octagonal floorplan with Gothic doorways and windows; unlike the Painshill temple, it is enclosed, giving greater scope for fine painted plasterwork in matt white and pastel shades. Its pedigree as a folly is further compounded by the existence of a basement room, accessed by an elaborate underground tunnel with a distant entrance set into the side of the hill. The idea was that servants could come and go without being seen by guests – which just goes to show that follies may be follies, but sometimes there really is method in the madness!

useful addresses

ADRIAN FISHER MAZES LTD Portman Lodge, Durweston, Dorset DT11 0QA Tel 01258 458845 www.mazemaker.com

ALICE IN WONDERLAND MAZE Merritown Lane, Hurn, Christchurch, Dorset Tel 01202 483444

BLENHEIM PALACE Woodstock, Oxfordshire Tel 08700 602080

CHATSWORTH HOUSE Bakewell, Derbyshire Tel 01246 565300

CHENIES MANOR HOUSE Chenies, Buckinghamshire Tel 01494 762888

ENGLISH HERITAGE Customer Services Department, PO Box 569, Swindon, Wiltshire SN2 2UR Tel 0870 333 1181

HALDON BELVEDERE Higher Ashton, Exeter, Devon Tel 01392 833668

HAMPTON COURT PALACE East Molesey, Surrey Tel 0870 752 7777

HATFIELD HOUSE Hatfield, Hertfordshire Tel 01707 262823

HEVER CASTLE Edenbridge, Kent Tel 01732 865 224

HOLYWELL BAY FUN PARK Newquay, Cornwall Tel 01637 830095

KENTWELL HALL Long Melford, Suffolk Tel 01787 310207

LAPPA VALLEY RAILWAY St Newlyn East, Newquay, Cornwall Tel 01872 510317

LEEDS CASTLE Maidstone, Kent Tel 01622 765400

LEGOLAND Windsor, Berkshire Tel 08705 040404

LONGLEAT HOUSE Warminster, Wiltshire Tel 01985 844400

THE MENAGERIE Horton, Northampton, Northamptonshire Tel 01604 870957

MOUNT EDGCUMBE COUNTRY PARK Cremyll, Torpoint, Cornwall Tel 01752 822 236

THE NATIONAL TRUST 36 Queen Anne's Gate, London SW1H 9AS Tel 0870 609 5380 (Greys Court, King Alfred's Tower, Saltram, Stourhead, Stowe, Wimpole Hall)

PAINSHILL PARK Portsmouth Road, Cobham, Surrey Tel 01932 864674

PARHAM PARK near Pulborough, West Sussex Tel 01903 742021

SONNING COMMON HERB FARM Peppard Road, Sonning Common. Reading, Berkshire Tel 0118 972 4220

TULLEY'S FARM Turners Hill Road, Turners Hill, Crawley, West Sussex Tel 01342 717071

WOOKEY HOLE CAVES Wookey Hole, Wells, Somerset Tel 01749 672243

index

A

Abberley Clock Tower 46, 47, 47
Adelaide, Queen 47
Alfred, King 50, 68
Alice in Wonderland Maze 40, 40
Alkborough Church window maze 10
Alkborough Maze 11
Anne, Queen 24
Archbishop's Maze 14, 15
Arthur, King 38
Astor, William Waldorf 23
Audley End 60, 60

B

Bacon, Francis 68
Barnard, Sir John 68
Bedford, Earl of 28
Black Prince, the 68
Blenheim, Battle of 24
Blenheim Palace 24
Boleyn, Anne 23
box 18, 28
Broadway Tower 64, 64
Brettingham, Robert William 60
Brown, 'Capablity' 20, 56

C

Castle Howard 72
Castle, The, Saltram 76, 76
Chatsworth House 26, 27
Chenies Manor House 28
Christian Church 10, 12, 16, 23, 50
Clavel's Folly 60, 61
Cobham, Lord 68
Coventry, 6th Earl of 64
Creech Grange Arch 59

D

Drake, Francis 68
Dudley, Earl of 47

E

Edgcumbe family 56
Edward I 26
Eleanor, Queen 26
Elizabeth I 50, 68
Ely Cathedral 16, 17
Elysian Fields 68, 72

F

Flitcroft, Henry 50, 66
Foley, Lord 47

G

George III 20, 60
Gibbons, Grinling 24
Gibbs, James 66
Gilbert Scott, Sir George 16
Glendurgan Garden 8–9
Gothic 46, 47, 52, 56, 64, 71, 76
Gothic Folly, Painshill 76, 77
Grass Bridge, Stourhead 67, 72, 73
Gresham, Sir Thomas 68

H

Haldon Belvedere 52, 52, 53
Halifax, 2nd Earl of 74
Hamilton, Charles 62
Hampden, John 68
Hampton Court Palace 20, 20
Hatfield House 18, 18, 19, 28, 29
Hengistbury Head 49, 49
Henry VIII 23, 62
herbs 18, 36
Hever Castle 22, 23
Hilton Turf Maze 11, 12
Horace 71
Horton House 74
House in the Clouds 48, 49
Hull, Richard 64

J

Jack the Treacle Eater's Tower 45
James I 60
Jerome, Jerome K. 20
Jones, Inigo 68
Jones, John 47

K

Kent, William 66
Kentwell Hall 23, 23
King Alfred's Tower, Stourhead 50, 50
King Arthur's Mirror Maze, Longleat 38, 38

L

labyrinths 10, 12, 16
Lappa Maze 34, 35
Lappa Valley Railway 34
Lawrence, Major-General Stringer 52
Leeds Castle 26, 26
Legoland 32, 32–33
Leith Hill Tower 64, 65
Locke, John 68
Locomotion 35
Longleat House 20, 21, 31, 38, 72

M

Marlborough, 1st Duke of 24
Marlborough Maze 24, 24, 25
Menagerie, The 74, 74, 75
Merlin's Magical Maze 32, 33
Middleton Arch 58, 59
Miller, Sanderson 56
Milton, John 68
Mount Edgcumbe Country Park, 56

N

Newton, Isaac 68

O

Octagon Lake, Stowe 72

P

Painshill Park 54, 55, 62, 62, 63, 76
Palk, Sir Robert 52
Palladian Bridge, Stowe 72, 72
Pantheon, Stourhead 67, 70, 71
Parham Park 40
Pope, Alexander 68
Poundbury 49

R

Raleigh, Walter 68
Richards, Reverend John 60
Rocket 35
Rousham Folly 59
Ruined Tower, Mount Edgcumbe Park 56, 56
Runcie, Archbishop Robert 12
Russell, Edward, Lord 28
Rustic Cottage, Stourhead 71, 71

S

Saltram 76
Saxons 36
Shakespeare, William 68
sham abbey, Painshill Park 62, 62, 63
sham castle, Ralph Allen's, Bath 42–43
sham castle, Wimpole Hall 56, 57
Sonning Common Herb Farm 36, 36
Spanish Succession, War of the 24
Sparrow, William 12
St Mary Redcliffe Church, Bristol 16, 16
Stephenson brothers 35

Stoke Newington Pumping Station 49
Stourhead 50, 67, 71
Stowe Landscape Gardens 6, 68, 71, 72
Styx, the 68

T

Temple of Apollo, Stourhead 71
Temple of Concord, Audley End 60, 60
Temple of Flora, Stourhead 71
Temple of the Sun, Stourhead 71
Temple of Worthies, Stowe 68, 68, 69
Tresham, Sir Thomas 50
Trevithick, Richard 35
Triangular Lodge, Rushton 50, 51
Tudors 18, 23, 28, 32
Tulleys Farm 36, 37
Turkish Tent, Painshill Park 55
Turner, J.M.W. 62

V

Vanbrugh, Sir John 24, 66
Veronica's Maze 40, 41

W

Watts Chapel 10, 16
William III (of Orange) 18, 20, 68
Wilton House 72
Wookey Hole Caves 38, 39
Wright, Thomas, of Durham 74
Wyatt, James 66
Wyck Rissington Church 16, 16

acknowledgments

Adrian Fisher is internationally recognized as the world's leading maze designer. He began designing mazes more than 20 years ago and has since created over 300 mazes in 17 countries across five continents. These include mazes that appear in this book at Greys Court, Wyck Rissington Church, Kentwell Hall, Blenheim Palace, Leeds Castle, Legoland Windsor, Holywell Bay Fun Park, Lappa Valley Railway, Sonning Common Herb Farm, Tulleys Farm, Longleat House, Wookey Hole Caves, Parham Park and the Alice-in-Wonderland Family Park. Adrian's deep appreciation for landscape, a love of history and the arts and an exceptional aptitude for tiling patterns and three-dimensional space all come into play in this unusual vocation.

Photographs are reproduced by kind permission of the following:

Devonshire Collection, Chatsworth, by permission of the Duke of Devonshire and the Chatsworth Settlement Trustees: p27; Adrian Fisher Mazes Ltd: pp21, 23, 32–3, 33 (below left), 36, 37, 38, 39, 40; Network/Dr Georg Gerster: 34–5; John Glover: pp19, 22, 41, 77; Jerry Harpur: pp18, 28, 29; Jarrold Publishing: p49 (by Esther Gumn); front cover, end papers (folly), pp1, 3, 7, 16 (below), 24, 42–3, 44, 45, 46, 47, 48, 50, 51, 52, 53, 56, 57, 58, 59, 60, 61, 62, 63, 64, 66, 67, 68, 69, 70, 71, 72, 73, 74, 75, 76 (by John Heseltine); The National Trust Photo Library: pp8–9, 14-15, 65, back cover; Dae Sasitorn/ lastrefuge.co.uk: p26; Jeff Saward/Labyrinthos: pp6, 10, 11, 12, 13, 16 (above), 17, 33 (below right); Skyscan Photolibrary: pp20, 25, 30, 31; Dawson Strange Photography: pp54, 55.

Labyrinth/maze artworks on end papers and page 26 by Mark Buckingham; page 12 by Mark Buckingham based on artwork supplied by Adrian Fisher Mazes Ltd.